The Battle

A mother's guide through anxiety, depression, and self-doubt.

Laura Mausolf

ISBN: 978-1986881579

This book is dedicated to all the moms out there kicking ass every day!

Contents

BE BRAVE: EXPLORE YOUR HISTORY .13

Step 1: Be Brave—Explore your history. 13

Being Brave: My Story 14

Chapter 1: ADVENTURES 25

Chapter 2: THOUGHTS 41

The Present 44

Your brain with anxiety and depression. 45

Steps to change your neuro-pathways 50

Step 1—Regular Exercise 50

Step 2—Practice meditation and mindfulness.

....52

Step 3—Practice appreciation! 54

Step 4—Put your phone, device, computer, or
iPad down! 56

Step 5—Laugh. 58

Step 6—Music..58

Steps I've successfully used to stop my negative thinking or panic in its tracks 61

Chapter 3: TRUTHS.............................65

Chapter 4: THE PAST 77

Letting go of Baggage..77

Learn to Delegate 86

Steps to improve your life today 86

Chapter 5: WHERE TO START? 93

Chapter 6: LIVING OUTSIDE YOUR COMFORT ZONE................................. 101

Exercises from Jenn Carrington 106

Is Ego Running Your Life?.................................108

Chapter 7: EVOLVE 115

Thought-Stream Exercise 118

How to Manifest What You Want in This Life. 123

Steps to Manifesting Your Wants 125

Chapter 8: THE BATTLE......................133

Chapter 9: WHEN THE SEASONS MESS WITH OUR BATTLE 137

Chapter 10: THE DAY-TO-DAY.............145
Top 3 Goals 155

RESOURCES...167

ACKNOWLEDGMENTS........................ 171

ABOUT THE AUTHOR 173

BE BRAVE: EXPLORE YOUR HISTORY.
> Step out of your comfort zone. Be open to transformation.

ADVENTURE: HOW'D WE GET HERE?
> Where do we want go next? Feel the fear and do it anyway!

THOUGHTS: CHANGE OUR MINDSET.
> Talk back to negative thoughts.

TRUTHS: MAKE NEW TRUTHS.
> Use positive affirmations to make a new story. Design a life you love!

LIVE: CREATE GOALS WITH ACTION STEPS.
> Do new things, take chances, and learn new skills.

EVOLVE: GROW, LEARN, AND FOLLOW YOUR DREAMS!
> Join our challenge group for love and support!

BE BRAVE FOR I KNOW
THE PLANS I HAVE FOR YOU.

declares the lord.

plans to prosper

and not harm you.

PLANS TO GIVE YOU
HOPE AND A FUTURE.

-jeremiah 29:11

BE BRAVE: EXPLORE YOUR HISTORY

I hope you are ready to do some hard work and to take an honest look at your life. Let's get you the life you want and deserve! Before we can start any work on any of the steps in The **B.A.T.T.L.E.** process, we have to start with where we have been. We need to take our life experiences and realize that both the good and bad experiences have made us into who we are today.

Step 1: Be Brave—Explore your history.

Take a moment before you dive in to this book. Reflect on the people, places, things, and events that have either helped or hindered where you are now. Write down the positive and negative moments that have made you who you are.

- Who or what influenced and shaped you into the person you have become?

- What events have influenced the path you have taken in life?

If there is anything on this list that negatively impacts how you feel or controls how you act today, cross them off. You no longer need to let past events control who you are today. They may have created you and impacted your experience, but you do not have to let them control you. Make a separate list of the negative things or events that have happened to you. In a safe setting, light them on fire and let them go. Say it aloud until you believe it.

"I have let you go!"

"You no longer control me."

Being Brave: My Story

Mom, mommy, mom, momma, mama, MMMMOOOOOOMMMM. Sounds familiar, huh?

It's OK if you just blocked me out. Ok, that was not very nice; you get enough of that at home. That is what my reality sounds like right now.

My name is Laura; I am a mom to two wild, energetic, crazy and sweet, loving boys. I love being a Mom. It is the thing I am most proud of in my life.

However, whether you are a new mom or a mom of five this parenting thing is not easy. Add worry, anxiety, or depression on to what you are already dealing with, and you feel easily overwhelmed and consumed with day-to-day life. We forget how to have fun and live a life we love.

If you want to learn how to cope with being a mother and having constant worry and anxiety, you are in the right place. I have found being brave and stepping out of my comfort zone are the best ways to overcome my doubts and fears.

I want to invite you to come on an adventure with me to be brave, whether you have suffered from anxiety and depression, or not. I want you to do the exercises, underline quotes you love, and write in it whenever you can. Otherwise, you'll put this book down because someone needs help and you'll forget that profound sentence you just read. This book will only be as good as the work you put into it. I know you are ready for changes because you are here. Things come into our life just when we need them. If this book has found you, pick it up, see where it will take you, and be ready to change your life.

My battle started when I was 14 and diagnosed with major depression disorder. Soon after, I developed an eating disorder and spent way too much time consumed with food. I felt out of control and this was the only control I had over my life. My mom could see I needed help and took me in to get it. I started to see a light at the end of the tunnel. Over the years, it has taken all my time, energy, and patience to love myself again. It took self-development, growth, research, and medication to finally be in a place where I feel I can help others in any stage of life. However, I am talking especially to those busy moms who are struggling because that's where I was and am in life. However, the teachings in this book can apply to ANYONE.

My passion for battling depression and helping other mothers continued after I experienced horrible postpartum depression with my first son, Easton. I should have been more aware of my increased susceptibility to post-partum depression because of my history. I got through it though, and so can you wherever you are on your journey. I always wished someone who had experienced depression would have been able to talk to me about it and help get me through it.

I had two older brothers and although I can now throw a solid punch, talking about feelings was not their forte. I did not have someone, but I would like to be that person for you, whatever stage of life you are at.

As time went on, I would often get calls from friends and family after they were trapped in that miserable place too; whether it was post-partum or any other time in their life. So many people are affected by mental stress. I soon realized that anxiety and depression are much more prevalent than we talk about and I should be sharing what I know with others who are stuck.

It's Not All Rainbows and Butterflies

Here's a glimpse into what my husband and I learned our first few months with a baby.

When we brought our first son home from the hospital, he was miserable. Pretty much everything that could go wrong did. He wouldn't nurse. I got mastitis, more than once. He didn't sleep and cried non-stop. My perfect little vision of life with a child quickly turned into a nightmare. We tried every formula, bottle, and pacifier known to mankind.

I pumped and tried nipple shields but it was unsuccessful. I tried to nurse repeatedly and I was distraught. I felt like a failure and was sure that being a Mom was my biggest failure yet. I clearly knew "breast is best", but sometimes it doesn't work. We need to be aware that it's OK and "fed is best." We should not be shaming mothers who choose to use formula because sometimes it's the only choice!

As someone with constant depression, I fell into severe postpartum depression and let me tell you: it was miserable. I didn't want visitors because I didn't want to worry that he was going to start screaming and not stop. I would sit on the edge of my seat waiting for him to cry while someone else held him. People would tell me to relax and go take a nap. I honestly would want to but was so overcome with anxiety that I couldn't. He cried for three months.

I brought him in to the pediatrician and they informed me, repeatedly, that he had colic. Until finally, he had blood in his poop. I say finally, because I now had concrete evidence that he was most definitely, not OK.

This went on until he was diagnosed with a milk-protein allergy. He had a pretty severe allergy, and we had to get a special formula that they use for NICU babies. Further examination revealed his liver enzymes were off and he was a bit anemic, but nothing too serious (at the time I did not feel that way, of course).

Let's face it; we all have a battle as parents. Kids are our greatest accomplishment and our hardest job. Sometimes things go as planned but more often than not, there are going to be roadblocks and challenging times.

Those are the times we have to stick it out and come together. As mothers, it is our job to do anything we can to keep our babies happy and healthy. To be successful at that—even to make a good effort at that—we need to do the same for ourselves.

My husband and I had to take four-hour shifts with earplugs and pillows over our heads to try to sleep and keep our cool. We had the TV cranked in our room while we took turns trying to sleep and we could still hear him crying. It broke our hearts, but there was nothing we could do until the milk protein was out of his system. "At least two weeks", they told us, until the protein would be out of his system and we would see improvement. But at least there was hope!

His butt was raw, bright red, and he had an open sore due to his allergy. We had to wrap him in a towel for a week straight to let the skin breathe and heal. Let me tell you, as a sleep-deprived mother, the last thing you want to do is wash poopy towels every day!

He even had an unresponsive episode where I gave my baby rescue breaths. We had been out at a fire station fundraiser and he was in his car seat, in the stroller. We were about to get in the car, but when I lifted him out, his body went limp. He was still pink and warm, but was dusky around his lips.

The nurse in me put him on the ground and I could feel a pulse. I put my lips over his little nose and mouth and gave him a breath. Suddenly, as if he had just held his breath for a long time, he inhaled and began to breathe normally.

He was fine one second, and the next he was not. I know God timed it perfectly so that it happened when I was able to see him instantly and do something about it. To this day, I don't know why this happened.

IT IS A BATTLE! We all have our own stressful events, at different levels of magnitude.

What's important is that my baby's butt healed, his stomach adjusted to the new formula, his liver enzymes returned to normal, and he started to thrive. He is now healthy, active, sweet, and sometimes, a pain in my ass. I would not have him any other way.

My biggest advice to any mom who feels an intense sadness and depression is to go in to see your doctor as soon as possible. Doctors do good screening for anxiety and depression.

But please answer those questionnaires honestly. If you don't, they can't help you to take care of yourself and your family. Also, you will find great support groups online if you have a child with a certain health concern or disease. Get the support you need to help you be the best mom you can be.

I promise you: Your biggest struggle will be your greatest accomplishment.

If you are someone who suffers with anxiety or depression, I strongly urge you to come up with a plan during pregnancy. Don't discount anti-depressants if you need them at any point in your life, even during pregnancy, but be sure to speak to a doctor instead of self-medicating, and follow your doctor's guidelines. If you need to add an anti-depressant at some point during your pregnancy, don't think of it as a failure. Think of it as a way to keep yourself healthy so you are able to take care of your baby and children. As mothers, we want to be perfect, but I have news for you: We never will be perfect—besides, perfect is boring. So, be OK with not being OK.

Don't let anyone shame you for needing medication—apparently, that is a thing now.

I cut down to the lowest dose possible during my pregnancy, but then increased my dose in my last trimester because I knew if I didn't, I wouldn't be able to take care of our baby. Everyone needs to decide what's best for him or her and for their baby, but when you become a mom, you must also be able to physically take care of another human. Make sure you are in the right frame of mind. If you are not feeling right after you have your baby, you need to see your doctor, as you would at any other time in your life.

After three months of misery and formula that cost $70 a can—that our doctor had to fight to get partial insurance coverage for—, our son ended up being super happy and smiley. Only then did I begin to see why people could have more than one child!

The moral of the story is to hang in there, Momma. It does get better and soon you will forget those sleepless nights. Well, maybe not forget, but they won't matter.

Once I went back to work, I started experiencing horrible anxiety. I chalked it up to being away from my baby and told myself to suck it up... and all the other things we tell ourselves.

Until one day, I felt like I couldn't breathe. I thought I was having an anxiety attack and asked one of the doctors to look at my throat to assure me I wasn't going crazy. Funnily enough, he looked at me and said that I had a goiter.

"You need to get your thyroid checked, ASAP."

He ordered labs for me, and they came back off the chart for hypothyroidism—low production of thyroid hormone, which can make you feel tired, affects mood and thinking, and contributes to depression. The most common cause is Hashimotos Thyroiditis, with which they later diagnosed me.

In patients with Hashimotos, the immune system's antibodies attack the thyroid, slowly destroying the cells that produce thyroid hormones.

The take away here is to make sure you don't have an underlying health condition that is contributing to making you feel like shit. If something feels wrong, act on your instinct. Don't let your negative self-talk convince you otherwise, or you will be unable to function as you should in every area of your life.

Learn from my mistakes!

So, what makes me think that I can help you with how you are feeling right now?

Because I have been there my friend!

I have been down ...way down... that black hole. I have struggled for twenty years; fighting my way out of that hole. After twenty years of research, self-help books, life struggles, and successes, I want to share my story and everything I have learned. I want to get you out of that dark and nasty place as quickly and simply as possible.

Chapter 1: **ADVENTURES**

What has brought you here? Where do you want to go?

Hopefully, you took a moment to look at where you have been and how you got there. I hope you were able to let go of the negative events in your life.

Now is the time to think about what brought you here to where you are right now, and what you are going to do to better yourself in order to get to where you want to be.

As moms, we are pulled in a million directions every day. We constantly run to and fro.

Guess what? We sometimes become tired, overwhelmed, and stressed out. Sometimes, life just feels like it is always taking from us and never giving back. We begin to feel overwhelmed by our day-to-day life, and we become stuck in a rut. Every day, more and more responsibilities are piled on our plate and we end up living for everyone else and forget to take care of ourselves.

If you are a new mom, I want you to take a deep breath and know that everything is going to be OK. Even when your precious bundle of joy is screaming for hours on end, remember that it is temporary, I promise.

For those of you who have kids that are growing into adults right before your eyes, take a deep breath, and know that everything is going to be OK.

- Maybe your son just let out a perfectly timed F-bomb in line at the store (yes that was my son). Let it go!

- Maybe you just screamed at your kids because it's the only way anyone will listen to you... Let it go!

- Permanent marker on your new floor? Let it go! (While the child offender is scrubbing said floor.)

- Your daughter just left the house on her first date? Let it go! Some things are beyond our control.

Let's be real and make sure we are taking the time we need to enjoy these years and be the best that we can be in a time full of uncertainty.

Let's explore why we feel so overwhelmed, and what we can do to release the anxiety and stress. If you suffer from constant worry, anxiety, depression, or self-doubt let's take a quick look at how we got here.

* * *

I want to take you on an adventure to release you from those thoughts of worry and get back to your life before you were overwhelmed with negative thoughts and self-doubt.

The Merriam Webster dictionary defines adventure as an exciting or remarkable experience, usually involving unknown risk. I hope I can excite you and get you back to the life you love even though you have struggles. Take a leap of faith and assume that doing the work in this book will be well worth the time and emotional investment.

I hope that at the end, you will feel like a weight has been lifted off your shoulders and you can start living the life you dream of. We can have—and indeed, we deserve—love, peace, and balance.

Have you ever experienced that overwhelming feeling of guilt, sadness, worry, anxiety, or worthlessness for no reason? Hell, maybe you have felt all of them.

Have your negative thoughts ever taken over your mind and refused to release their grips on you? Has life ever seemed too much, or have you felt that maybe you are just not good enough? You can't sleep, focus, or enjoy the things that used to bring you joy?

Chances are that you have had these feelings and thoughts before. And perhaps, you have them right now. If any of this resonates with you now or at any point in your life, we can start implementing exercises and practices to change your mind-set. Your mind controls your emotions, which then controls your response to external influences around you. Nurturing the mind is the key to success and happiness.

We will explore motherhood and how we tend to stop serving ourselves. It is in doing so that we disconnect from our higher self, or the universe, or God.

We all have this highly creative place in our brain that lives in the moment and enjoys life. This is where we are able to connect on a different level.

I don't care if you want to call it instinct, God, your higher self, or your true self. It doesn't matter what you call it. You can call it all of them—that is not what is important. But it is important that you recognize that it's there.

Please don't worry about the terminology, because if you do, you're going to miss the point of this book. Let that go and focus on growing and learning.

We have so much to learn while our children grow from infants to adults. Starting with the day they are born you're constantly questioning whether you are doing things correctly. Add in the stacks of instructions containing do's and don'ts from the hospital and you can easily start to second-guess your intuition.

I am here to tell you that if your kids are safe and taken care of, you can put all the literature down and simply enjoy the kids. Of course, listen to what your doctors say, but don't discount your intuition.

I am going to tell you right now that I am not a psychiatrist, therapist, or a doctor of any kind. All of the work and words in this book come from my own experiences, research, and self-development that I have collected over the years.

I can tell you I am a R.N. that has worked in the emergency department and I have seen the reality of life with mental illness.

I truly live to serve others. I am a nurse by trade and love the time I spend with patients while helping them through critical times in their life. I felt an urge to write this book to help others in a different way. I will list some resources and books that have helped me at the end of this book, if you want to expand your sense of self.

If you are waiting for an invitation to change your life, this is it. You are already doing it.

It's not hard to get lost, because mothers tend to put everyone's needs in front of our own. I want you to look at who YOU are for a change. What if you started exploring things YOU wanted to do? Then you look at the spectrum of personalities in our society today, you will see angry, skeptical people who believe the world is out to get them. They feel the world owes them something and when they don't magically get it, they believe nothing is possible.

This is proof that if you look for failure, you will find it. If you look for reasons why something won't work, you will find excuses not to try.

On the other side of the spectrum, people live with a false sense of self and spend their time portraying who they want to be, but they are living in a false reality. I am not judging here. I can appreciate that I do not experience what they do.

There must be some middle ground for the rest of us, right?

Most of us lie somewhere between these extremes. Those who just want to be happy and enjoy our husbands, kids, and life. What if we took a moment to think as we did when we were kids—when we just did what made US happy?

What if we lived from the inside out, doing the things we love and that excite us; instead of bringing the outside influences in and letting others dictate who we should be. The answers to these questions are what we should be doing in some form or another.

Suppose we move away from all the external influences that tell us we need to consume for people to like us, or to be successful. What if we looked at life as we did when we were children, before outside influences told us we were not good enough? Somewhere along the line, we changed our thinking from what made us happy to worrying about what other people would think about us. What if we focused on working on ourselves? You are what you love, not what loves you.

After living in a place of being disconnected from our true self, we develop this nasty, negative self-talk. This grows to worry, anxiety, depression and self doubt. And all of these things hold you back. They hold you back personally, professionally, as a wife, mother, and friend.

Let's figure out why anxiety and depression rule your world and how you can get your life back on track. The first step in doing so is making decisions for you, and not what the rest of the world will think.

When we focus on the impulses, stressors, and demands life places on us as caretakers in an overly stimulated world, we forget that we have a voice. The stress of the daily grind has chewed us up and spit us out. We are not meant to live life miserable.

I'm not sure when we decided we were OK with mediocre. We all have amazing gifts to share. When we leave the things that matter most at the bottom of our priority lists, we are absolutely not in touch with our inner selves. We start living a life we have not designed; a life we did not imagine, and a life that does not suit our life designs.

We spend our time searching for the life we believe we are missing. We are left hanging on every day, struggling to keep our heads above water.

* * *

So, why do some people have it all together?

It is interesting that some seem to have it all: all the luck, success, fortune, and opportunities. Meanwhile, we are treading water, and can slowly feel our heads going under. We are running on our last bit of adrenaline and we need something to change.

First of all, looks can be deceiving. Everyone has his or her own difficulties and setbacks and the worst thing we can do is to compare ourselves to ANYONE else. As my mentor, Natasha Hazlett would say, STAY IN YOUR OWN GOD DAMN LANE! I promise you this: that mom who seems to have life organized and perfect in every way, is probably overcompensating. She is probably exhausted each day from spending her days trying to uphold a certain standard for fear of what everyone else might think of her.

So, from now on, the new rules are:

- QUIT COMPARING

- BE A NICE HUMAN

- SERVE OTHERS

- LOOK AFTER EACH OTHER

- LIVE THE LIFE YOU LOVE.

As mothers, we should be lifting each other up by sharing our stories. We should not be hiding behind Facebook, wishing we had real friends. We should be having coffee, play dates, and looking forward to spending time with someone.

Say YES to things you normally wouldn't. The trick is to enjoy yourself and quit comparing your husband, kids, and life to that of others. Just STOP! Comparison is the thief of joy.

You've heard that saying: "It takes a village." We need to get back to looking at life that way instead of thinking we should do everything ourselves.

We "should" do many things. I should do this, I should do that... Remove the word "should" from your vocabulary today and try "being" instead.

Start taking notice of the things around you in each moment of the day. Use your senses to stay in the now. This will help you enjoy the here and now instead of looking ahead where you need to go or looking back at mistakes you have made.

Do we focus on the negatives or positives in life? We all have challenges, trauma, difficulties, struggles, and problems but how we deal with the cards we are dealt—our MINDSET—is how we change the game.

No one's shit is bigger or "badder" than another person's is, because in the end, bad things happen to all of us. We have to find a way not to focus on them. Push them out of the way, and carry on.

* * *

Free yourself from the worry, anxiety, and depression that hold you back. Sometimes, the only way to do that is to feel the fear, acknowledge that it is there, and do it anyway. You are exactly where you belong. I'm going to teach you and help you practice and win the MINDSET game.

"FEEL THE FEAR AND DO IT ANYWAY."

This is not an easy journey. You will have work to do—hard work. You may have to confront things from your past that you have swept way, way under that rug. Don't worry though; you don't have to stay there long before you can move on to becoming the best you—the you that you know you are meant to be. The you from a different time, before the pressures and influences of others brought you down to where THEY thought you were supposed to be.

It doesn't matter what we have done in the past or who we were. We can let that go. I am telling you to let that guilt go, right now. You get a clean slate. It is not serving you or your family to be holding on to that crap.

There will be exercises that can help you transform your life. If you complete the challenges at the end of each chapter, you will transform your life. If you take the time and put in the work now, you will be rewarded. Your life will start to look up, things will fall in to place, and your fear and anxiety will be lifted, improving your depression or negative state of mind.

What do you have to lose?

We all have a story, we all have baggage, we are all capable of changing and become the best version of OURSELVES.

RULE
YOUR
mind
or it
will
rule
YOU.
-BUDDHA

Chapter 2: THOUGHTS

Mindset seems to be a buzzword lately. But how do we incorporate that in to our life as a mother?

When we are constantly worrying about others, we forget to check our own selves. We become so stuck on checking on our children and maybe even husbands, but forget to check on ourselves.

Think of yourself like a CEO. You have to pay yourself first to keep the company up and running, then you can pay everyone else. Make deposits into YOUR account so you don't go under. The quickest and easiest way to do this is to check your mindset.

Mindset is your attitude, outlook, mentality, and approach to life. If you are in the right mindset, you can accomplish things you wouldn't normally take on.

Growing up, we are taught that we can't do things because they are too dangerous, too expensive, or too challenging. We learn to say "no" and we learn to quit because there seems to be no point to putting in the effort if we know we can't do it or be the best.

That's what we teach OUR kids! Good grief! No wonder the world is such a mess.

I can't count the number of times I have told my own sons "no" in their short little lives. What if we didn't play safe? What if we played big? What if we changed our mindset from average is good, to average is not acceptable to me or for my family? Our mindset is conditioned to think that if we do enough, then that is what we were made for. What if we changed our mindset by using a vision?

Forgetting our lack of confidence and limited belief. What if we could identify our direction and purpose? If you are tired of more of the same, it is time to become *intentional* with what you want and tell the *universe* that you want it.

Keep that in the back of your mind when you are constantly telling your child their dreams are not realistic. Or when we downplay their thoughts and ideas. Think about how that will affect them in the future.

What do you want to do with your life? What would change your life? What is important to you?

Take time to think about a vision you could work towards. Your dreams, goals, wants and desires. Put them in the blank space below. If you want to take it a step further make a vision board. I suggest making one on your phone and setting it to your back drop! Every time you turn your phone on you are reminded about your wants and desires!

* * *

We can design our life.

We need to:

- Have a purpose,
- Live intentionally,
- Believe in ourselves,
- Be open to opportunities,
- Listen and take action. . .

The Present

You do not have to have an official diagnosis; we all experience overwhelming emotions on some level in our life. We are stressed to the max with family life, work, trying to be a good wife, parent—the Perfect Pinterest Mom. We try to lead the cub scouts, make the treats for the bake sale, pick up friends' kids for baseball, and return to school to better ourselves. It is exhausting!

We try to do it all. We try to balance this plate with these activities and commitments.

The problem is the plate is on a burning stick, we are balancing on a ball, with one foot, and we have snot and food on our scrubs or work shirts while we are doing it. It's time to take it down a notch. We have lost sight of why we are doing this all in the first place.

We do NOT have to be the best; we can ask for and accept help, buy the Valentines for school from the damn store if you need to and throw in a bag of fruit snacks. Use the people around you to help lift you up and—for God's sake—if you have a newborn, find some mommas who you can meet up with for your sanity's sake. If you are new to an area, look for a local mom group and meet some new friends.

If you have been fighting anxiety and depression your whole life like me, or you're newly diagnosed and you're not sure what to expect—or you're just freakin' stressed out and can't seem to find that person you once were—let me tell you, my friend, you are here now.

Take a deep breath and know things will now start to get better from this moment. Seriously, say that aloud: Things will be better starting now!

This can be a difficult and challenging time, but if you learn what's happening inside your head and how it affects your body, you stand a much better chance of living an amazing life.

Let's talk about worry and anxiety a little bit, so you understand what's happening in the brain when you are feeling overwhelmed because there is just too much to handle in your life.

Your brain with anxiety and depression.

OK, so you may not find this is the most mind-blowing or exciting stuff, but I feel like it is important we understand the anatomy and physiology of our brain and why we end up with obsessive worry, anxiety, and depression in the first place. We need to know where we are currently in order to adjust the course and work towards our goals. Plus, the nurse in me loves this, so hang in there.

According to the National Institute of Mental Health, 40 million adults in the US alone, have an anxiety disorder—that's about 18% of the population, my friends. Nearly thirty-seven percent of these people are receiving treatment, such as psychotherapy (otherwise known as talk therapy), exposure therapy, or medication. It can of course also be a mix of more than one of those things, as is usually recommended. Perhaps we need to consider mental health in the United States and the resources we have to serve those who need it—or rather, the lack of mental health resources. Our system is so broken. We need to make it better; I intend to make this my life goal!

Pair a broken system where we are short psychiatrists, physicians, social workers, nurses, and support of any kind, with a nation that does not acknowledge mental health as a crisis, and we find ourselves in the mess we are in.

Soldiers come home from the front lines where they watched friends die, or where they had to kill people. When they come home, they can no longer comprehend the world we live in.

We do not have the ability to care for them in a timely manner. They usually receive bags of medication (lots of medication) and are sent home. No wonder they start to look for other ways to ease their pain and suffering. This is actually my friend's experience. Not only did he have to readjust to the world around him, but also no one gave a shit.

My friends, we need to care and start looking after one another. We need to change our self-serving thinking and start finding ways to serve others.

Anxiety and depression start when we develop irrational thoughts and draw conclusions from these thoughts. We separate logic and act on feelings, and in our minds, we start to mix the two up. This can lead to the symptoms we know of: the inability to focus, tremors, racing thoughts, self-doubt, worry, and insomnia—or on the flip side, sleeping too much. This can lead to anxiety, depression, even self-harm or suicide.

* * *

When this happens, our bodies produce cortisol and adrenaline, which ignite a fight or flight response. The sympathetic nervous system is responsible for causing most of the physical symptoms associated with anxiety. This response is what our bodies are supposed do when we feel threatened. The problem is that the body doesn't realize we are not cave men any more. We are not running from Saber Tooth Tigers—lucky for us—but our bodies still respond the same way internally.

This response to continuous stress, left uncontrolled, can lead to mental stress. When our bodies are constantly in a state of being ready to fight, it can lead to an overproduction of cortisol, which wreaks havoc on your body. This reaction is characterized by a rapid heart rate, increased physical energy, dilated pupils, sharpened senses, and a racing mind.

This physical response can be beneficial when we are faced with danger, but when we are in this state for long periods; it is detrimental to our functioning. If we encounter this anxiety repeatedly, it can lead to increased blood pressure, fatigue from living in a state of high alert, tremors, sweating, tingling, vomiting, chest pain, and shortness of breath.

After working in an ER, I can tell you that chest pain and shortness of breath can mimic a heart attack. You still should see a doctor if these symptoms persist.

During times of serious and prolonged stress, the brain develops neuro-pathways in which our thoughts and feelings are fired repeatedly along the same "roads" or pathways. The synaptic connections become easier to fire, and like most things, will follow the path of least resistance. The more we continue to have these irrational and negative thoughts, the quicker and easier it is for this pathway to be activated. Unless we take a moment to tell ourselves to stop the negative thoughts, they come more frequently and with little difficulty.

The good news is that we can actually "reroute" those pathways. We can do this because of the brain's neuroplasticity; that is, the brain's ability to restructure itself by forming new neural connections throughout our life.

To help shut down the negative pathways (our negative self-talk) from firing, we have to fight back. We need to stop the firing off the negative pathways. Once activated, the pathways are more receptive to signals. This increases the repetitive thoughts that lead to feelings of self-defeat and if continued, mental disorders.

We need to think about what is going on between our ears. We have to have an active plan to change the pathways and reduce the amount of cortisol and adrenaline we produce on a daily basis. This neuroplasticity is what will lead us to new and healthier thoughts. Here are some tried-and-true methods I have found through personal experience, self-development, and research.

* * *

Disclaimer: I do have to mention that if at any time, if you feel suicidal, unsafe, or unstable, you need to seek expert care and get help right away. There's no shame in asking for help.

* * *

Steps to change your neuro-pathways

Here are things you can do right now to FEEL better instantly. I realize these are things you may have heard before, but I want you to look at doing them to shut down those negative pathways so you can start feeling better as soon as possible.

Step 1—Regular Exercise

I know this is not rocket science for anyone, but the hard part is getting up and doing the work. Knowing that exercise will reduce your cortisol levels and stress is usually not enough to get us motivated, until we do it and feel the effects.

Once you start doing it, you will notice your body will crave it. Your body will not feel the need to produce more cortisol and your extra anxiety or energy will be burned off. You might gain self-confidence as you see your body change in response to the exercise.

To help get you started, try finding an account-ability partner who will join you in going for a walk, start a group fitness class, or ANYTHING to get you moving!

Start small if you must, but just start.

What can you do at the office or at home with the baby? I was pretty awesome at doing squats with my babies. Get creative. Take a walk around the block with a friend. Find someone who WILL HOLD you accountable, by calling you out on your bullshit when you try to talk yourself out of going. That's the person you need for this, not the friend who will say "better luck next time"!

Find a gym you like. I hate going to a packed yoga studio. I went once and found myself staring at someone's crotch or butt the whole time. I have learned over the years that I am an independent exerciser. If that's you, put some headphones in, crank up the tunes, and ignore the rest.

Not ready to go to the gym? Try some light stretching at home. There are also a bazillion exercise videos online for free right at your fingertips. Utilize your resources.

Step 2—Practice meditation and mindfulness.

If this is new to you and seems like a little bit too much, I'm begging you to try it.

Meditation will help you:

- focus your mind

- think clearly

- and find an emotionally calm place.

If you are really feeling up for it, attempt to practice guided meditation. Lookup some guided meditations online—I know you'll find a ton of them. Check Out Joseph Clough's App!

Pick one and go for it. Don't over think it, although I know you will, because that's what we do.

Meditation is incredible for changing our brain and the ways we think. Talk about retraining your brain and neural pathways, this is a great way to do it. Try to do guided meditation a couple times a week and see the impact it will have on your mindset.

The best way to make sure you get it done is to do it at bedtime. When you lay down for the night, start to focus on your breath. Feel your breath going in your nostrils for a count of four, into your lungs for four, and out of your mouth for another four.

Let the stress of the day melt away as you inhale for four seconds, hold your breath for four seconds, and let it go for four seconds.

When you breathe in, pick an uplifting or inspirational word like hope, light, energy, love, confidence, or strength. When you breathe in, repeat this word in your head, or out loud, and think about breathing this word in. Hold it with you for those four seconds.

When you breathe out for those four seconds, think of letting go. Pick a word you could use less of; like fear, anxiety, worry, anger, resentment; anything you want to let go of.

Once you hold your breath for four seconds, exhale, and think about letting that word go.

Example:

- Inhale love for a count of one....2....3....4....

- Now hold love in your heart and let go of worry for a count of one...two...three...four...

Do that every night and you will be well on your way to a healthier mindset.

Step 3—Practice appreciation!

Appreciate family, friends, your neighborhood barista, nature, scenery, and people—anything around you. Send thoughts of gratitude out to the world and see what the universe delivers to you. This can be as simple as stating your gratitude to your beautiful garden and picking something specific you love about it. Continue this practice throughout the day and watch how good things will naturally and easily come your way.

Now I don't expect you to be living in sugar-plum-and-gumdrop land, but if you can take a moment for appreciation each day, your mind map will begin to change and the universe will notice.

There is scientific proof that being grateful impacts the brain. Psychology Today has an article by Alex Korb, Ph.D. in which he states that practicing gratitude can help you lower anxiety and depression. Here's a link for the article. Alex Korb, The Greatful Brain Article. It can also help you exercise more, sleep better, and be happier. Gratitude requires you to appreciate the positive aspects in your life and it is not comparing yourself to others.

You actually have to show appreciation for what you have.

Dr. Korb continues by explaining evidence that people who showed more gratitude had higher levels of activity in the hypothalamus. You should care about this because the hypothalamus controls a large portion of our bodily functions, including eating, drinking, and sleeping. It influences your metabolism and stress levels.

Appreciation + gratitude = better appetite, healthier habits, and improved sleep quality. These things will help you live a healthier and happier life.

Step 4—Put your phone, device, computer, or iPad down!

Turn your TV off and do something you love. Unplug from the constant bombardment of ads, negative messages, and Facebook chain mail. If you want to talk to someone, pick up your phone and call them.

Do we even know how to do this anymore?

Have we lost ourselves to emojis? (Guilty!)

This is a work in progress for me currently.

Have you ever been to a restaurant where everyone at the table is on the phone and NO ONE is looking up?

How often do we even make eye contact with the waitress?

Start with an easy fix. Are phones allowed during family dinner? Consider placing a basket on the counter where the phones have to go during mealtimes and use this time to connect as a family. Yes, even us moms!

Writing this book gave me a great opportunity to do a lot of research. Unfortunately, I was on my phone much more than I normally am. It was clear to see that my boys felt the need to compete for my attention every time I took my phone out. If I took a moment to explain to them what I was doing, and why I was spending time on the phone instead of with them, they usually understood—as long as it was temporary.

Now, if you are watching Facebook cat videos and could actually be interacting with them, you should be doing THAT! I'm not judging. As I said, the phone thing is a work in progress for me, which is why I'm there to support you.

Impact of the Internet on Mental Health

We are surrounded by social connectivity everywhere on the Internet and this can lead to isolation, which might trigger mental health issues, especially in our adolescent population where connected devices tend to take us down slippery slopes.

We can have a conversation with someone across the country we have never met, but we can't have an open and honest conversation with our spouse sitting next to us. Open your mouth and attempt to have the dialog. It might be clumsy and awkward at first, but it will get easier with time. You might even find you enjoy each other!

If you don't know what you love or forgot your passion somewhere in that mountain of diapers and laundry, don't worry. I will help you find that in the exercise at the end of the chapter.

Step 5—Laugh.

Connect with others who you know you enjoy. Go out for coffee, lunch, or a walk. Spend time asking them questions; share with them what's going on, and most importantly—have fun and laugh.

Bring back the art of conversation without emojis. Don't forget it's OK to laugh at yourself, as long as you are not beating yourself up. Give yourself some grace, especially if you send your kids to school and they have the day off. It's OK to laugh and not be so serious all the time.

Step 6—Music.

Music has been proven to improve moods and reduce stress. Find something that you can relate to and that you enjoy. Take some time to blast it on the radio and maybe even dance. Include your family in the process and watch how much fun you will all have. Be silly, have fun, and let yourself enjoy life! It's ok, you can, and I give you permission!

Perhaps the best thing we can do to start living and feeling better today, is to pay attention to your negative thoughts. These are the thoughts that are constantly ruminating through our head all day.

Did you know you were even having them? That's the worst part; most of the time we don't even realize it. These thoughts are running loose, causing chaos in our lives and we have no idea why we are so miserable when 60,000 times a day, we tell ourselves we are worthless, unable, not educated enough, not outgoing enough, not pretty enough and on and on.

This is what is happening now, but we can make it a point to address the fact that these are just THOUGHTS and not TRUTHS. You can learn to stop these thoughts in an instant and create a positive thought to put in its place even if you don't believe it at first.

If you can live your life, believing that crazy madness you make up, you might as well make it good!

Our minds start racing and making up completely fake stories and we start believing them. We need to recognize that these negative thoughts are just that—*thoughts*.

When you catch yourself thinking something unpleasant, take a moment to address the thought by saying to yourself: *I realize this is just a thought and I choose not to believe it.* You can also call it a red flag.

You can call out the red flag and change it to a positive thought (or a green flag) to correct and replace those negative thoughts.

Catch the red flag, (negative thoughts) and replace them with a green feel-good thought.

Example: *I'm calling you out (red flag), my thought of not being good enough to try a new job and I am calling bullshit. I am smart and capable enough to rock this new gig! (green flag)*

If you know the negative thoughts you repeat over and over, have a green flag thought ready to go when the red flag flies up. That way you are prepared and don't have to over think it.

Steps I've successfully used to stop my negative thinking or panic in its tracks

Again—always a work in progress for me.

One. As soon as you notice the negative thought, picture a huge stop sign; bright red with blinking lights around it! Or a Red flag. Can you see it? OK, good! As soon as you see the stop sign or red flag, tell that thought to STOP and go to step two.

Two. Ask yourself: is this thought true? Am I being threatened? Is there actually a lion chasing me down the street? If not, you know it's OK to put up your red flag and stop the negative thoughts before you send yourself into panic mode.

Three. Change the story. Tell yourself: *Thank you for trying to keep me safe but I got this!* Try to have a go-to positive thought ready in your head. Keep it simple but believable. For example: *I am enough. This is not a big deal. The universe has my back. Thanks for trying to help, but I got this! I appreciate you looking out for me, but I'm ready to do this!*

You can use this with your kids too. When they start reacting to something, ask them if this is a little problem or a big problem. It helps things seem less intense and scary and helps them put things in to perspective.

REMEMBER HER?

she is still there...inside you...waiting
let's go get her

Chapter 3: **TRUTHS**

Do you remember who you are without all of those negative thoughts? Do you even know who you are or what you are about? Who are you at your core? What do you stand for besides your family? What are the values that you live your life by?

No matter what happens, those things will usually come first. I want you to take a moment and think about the things you think you value in life. What are the values that influence the way you live and make decisions? Are these the values you want to live your life by?

When we are suffering from constant negative thinking, anxiety, and depression, we sometimes lose sight of who we are and what matters most to us. We become consumed with this black cloud that hangs over us. We cannot describe it to those who do not understand, but we just know we feel horrible. We feel like we have done something wrong and we are consumed with doubt and guilt over nothing and everything. We can't focus, everything is suddenly overwhelming. We are doing fine and then one day—BAM!—it hits us.

It is time to lift that cloud and start getting back to the person we know we can be and who we were before we were dealing with anxiety and depression.

Values guide us in our decisions, behaviors, and actions. If you know what you value, life can be more satisfying and enjoyable. You can use these values to help guide you when making decisions. When you make decisions that are not in line with our values, you will feel internal tension. This in turn can cause your anxiety to flare up.

So how do we know what our values are?

- What do you have to experience in life to feel fulfilled?

    o What makes you excited and amped up?

    o What gets your blood pumping and you start to feel giddy inside like a little kid?

- What values do you need to honor or a part of you weakens?

- Can you group some of your values together to come up with one centralized theme for them?

- Your values should encourage you, cause an emotional response, and be meaningful to you so you are inspired to maintain them every day.

I want you to take time and think about the words in the list below carefully. Which ones stand out? Go through them and circle everyone that you can relate to, or which lines up with your thoughts and beliefs. If you are not sure, circle the ones you want to have from now going forward.

VALUES

Acceptance	Family	Productivity
Accountability	Famous	Professional
Accuracy	Fearless	Prosperity
Achievement	Feelings	Purpose
Alertness	Ferocious	Quality
Altruism	Fidelity	Realistic
Ambition	Focus	Reason
Amusement	Foresight	Recognition
Assertiveness	Fortitude	Recreation
Attentive	Freedom	Reflective
Awareness	Friendship	Respect
Balance	Fun	Responsibility
Boldness	Generosity	Restraint
Bravery	Genius	Results-oriented

VALUES

Brilliance	Giving	Reverence
Calm	Goodness	Rigor
Candor	Grace	Risk
Capable	Gratitude	Satisfaction
Careful	Greatness	Security
Certainty	Growth	Self-reliance
Challenge	Happiness	Selfless
Charity	Hard work	Sensitivity
Cleanliness	Harmony	Serenity
Clear	Health	Service
Clever	Honesty	Sharing
Comfort	Honor	Significance
Commitment	Hope	Simplicity
Common sense	Humility	Sincerity

VALUES

Communication	Imagination	Skill
Community	Improvement	Skillfulness
Compassion	Independence	Smart
Competence	Individuality	Solitude
Concentration	Innovation	Spirit
Confidence	Inquisitive	Spirituality
Connection	Insightful	Spontaneous
Consciousness	Inspiring	Stability
Consistency	Integrity	Status
Contentment	Intelligence	Stewardship
Contribution	Intensity	Strength
Control	Intuitive	Structure
Conviction	Irreverent	Success
Cooperation	Joy	Support

VALUES

Courage	Justice	Surprise
Courtesy	Kindness	Sustainability
Creativity	Knowledge	Talent
Credibility	Lawful	Teamwork
Curiosity	Leadership	Temperance
Decisiveness	Learning	Thankful
Dedication	Liberty	Thorough
Dependability	Logic	Thoughtful
Determination	Love	Timeliness
Development	Loyalty	Tolerance
Devotion	Mastery	Toughness
Dignity	Maturity	Traditional
Discipline	Meaning	Tranquility
Discovery	Moderation	Transparency

VALUES

Drive	Motivation	Trust
Effectiveness	Openness	Trustworthy
Efficiency	Optimism	Truth
Empathy	Order	Understanding
Empower	Organization	Uniqueness
Endurance	Originality	Unity
Energy	Passion	Valor
Enjoyment	Patience	Victory
Enthusiasm	Peace	Vigor
Equality	Performance	Vision
Ethical	Persistence	Vitality
Excellence	Playfulness	Wealth
Experience	Poise	Welcoming
Exploration	Potential	Winning

VALUES

Expressive	Power	Wisdom
Fairness	Present	Wonder

Reference—Heather Quisel—Level Up Your Life!

Whew! Did you make it? That's a lot of values! So, now you have a great start to what matters most to you! Look at that list. It's time to make some cuts, when you are ready.

Now, of all the values you narrowed down, which ones speak to you?

Can you combine a few that all represent the same thing?

Come up with the ten that speak to you and encompass who you are and what you represent.

Why are we working so hard on our values? Before we can go any further in who we want to be and who we want to become, we need to know what we represent and who we want to be.

Now take that top 10 and pick your top five most important values. This should be fun and inspiring!

Once you have you top five, circle them, rewrite them, and post them up where you can see them every day.

Use your values to help you make difficult decisions every day. Just ask yourself which options align most with your values. If it doesn't align with your values, it's probably not a good idea and is just going to increase your anxiety and make you feel bad about yourself.

The great news is that you are one-step closer to your true self. These values can help you create a bulletproof belief system. Own them and be ready to play for keeps! Game on!

BE YOURSELF; EVERYONE
else is already taken.
-oscar wild

Chapter 4: THE PAST

Letting go of Baggage

Life has its ups and downs. We live and learn and we move on—at least, that's what is supposed to happen.

Sometimes in life, we are dealt a shitty hand, we make bad choices, we enter toxic relationships and start pretending to be someone we are not. It's OK to have baggage—we all do!—but if we are still carrying it around and letting it affect our day-to-day life, it's time to do some work, my friend. Seriously, it's time to lift that ton of bricks off your shoulders. See ya! Don't let the door hit you in the ass on the way out!

The past is the past for a reason. We cannot change it, no matter how much we wish we could. Think about how much our lives could improve if we were to focus on the here and now.

What if we could wake up in the moment and let go of the grief, shame, and depression of the past? What if we could focus on now and not worry about the future. Worry is stealing your energy. There is nothing there of value. What could you do or create if you were in the here and now every day?

I have made many mistakes my life and holding on to them has severely impacted how I showed up to my life and to the world. As soon as I could release the baggage with the exercise at the end of this chapter, I was able to move on. I felt free. I physically felt like a weight was lifted off my shoulders. Do the work here—it's hard but worth it.

When you can let go of the hurt, shame, guilt, bad choices and mistakes and know that you have learned from them, you can move on with your life with no regrets. These are what help us figure out what we don't want in life, and we can use that to figure out what we DO want instead.

For example, I drank a lot in college. Part self-medicating and part of it was that I felt lost. I ended up with drinking tickets, which progressed to a DUI, and eventually, I woke up in jail one day. I had a cell mate with the word "rainbow" tattooed on her arm; she had purple and black hair and she had a tough life. She was sent for me by the universe.

After talking to her, I knew I had to change my life. If I had not met her and had that conversation in that jail cell, I would have kept going down that path of destruction. Life changed for me that day, and I vowed to have a purpose from there on in. Soon after, I enrolled in nursing school and met my husband. Coincidence? No such thing!

Here is what I want you to ask yourself: Who are you still pretending to be?

We all develop masks in life. These masks we develop when we endure trauma, struggle, hurt, or a series of negative events. The masks help us cope and keep us safe. They are a safety mechanism. People don't get to see the real us. We keep that hidden inside until we know it's safe to take our masks off.

Our masks can change our behavior and how we interact with those around us. What we don't know is that people can usually tell when we are wearing a mask. They maybe don't know what it is, but people take notice when we are not being our authentic selves.

Our challenge is to decide what masks we are wearing. What masks have we developed over the years that keep us safe?

I myself have been a queen people pleaser. I go out of my way to help people even if it means putting my ideas or to do list on hold. I will go out of my way to help someone who has treated me poorly. Now this can be okay, but we can't go through life not focusing on the things we want and love to do. It is great to help people obviously but be careful where you draw that boundary line and when it gets crossed. As you start working on yourself and bettering yourself, you may find that others may be against it and try to take you off course. Just stay focused on where you are trying to go.

Wearing these masks is exhausting and it keeps us from living our authentic life. What would happen if we were to lower our mask or even take it off?

You can keep it on standby if you need it, but is it still SERVING you? Oftentimes, we are still wearing masks that we developed as a child or adolescent, and it may or may not be serving you today. As adolescents, we try out different masks to see what fits. Or we may wear a mask to fit in.

It's time to just be ourselves and not care what everyone else thinks. Trust me; I know this is so much easier said than done!

You may be wearing a mask without even realizing it! Has a hurtful comment ever come out of your mouth, on the defense, and you didn't even realize it? Later, you feel horrible that you were such an asshole. You are left wondering why you said what you did... It's your mask! Your masks help guard your emotions. Other masks can include self-criticizing before others can criticize you, lack of confidence, people pleasing, perfectionism, over indulging (food, shopping, gambling, alcohol).

Let's look at why these are not helping you. If you are wearing masks, you are not letting people meet and see the real you. Guarding your emotions will not let others in to develop significant relationships with you. You may come off as distant or cold when you don't need to shield yourself anymore.

These masks—more than anything else—show us that we love control. If we have control, we don't get hurt or taken advantage of. If you want to be your best self, you have to let your guard down.

Try having an open heart and think of how you can help others by being of service to others. We must be have an open heart that's free of baggage. That will only hold us back.

So, now is the time to ask yourself: Can I take my mask off? Know if you feel you need to, you can put the mask back on.

If you have been hurt in the past, consider that LIFE HAPPENS FOR YOU NOT TO YOU!

In everything you have experienced—good or bad—, what can you take from it and learn? What was—or is—the universe trying to teach me? What can I carry forward to make me a better, smarter person?

When we let go of our masks, we need to let the baggage that came with those masks go as well. When we can do that, we can also let go of the doubts of others that we may have picked up. The doubts we listen to and then think they are our truths, when in fact; they are other's insecurities being projected on to us. You do not need to indulge and take those thoughts as your truths.

I spent a lot of time in my life pleasing others and paying more attention to what others thought of me than what I really wanted. I allowed that to stop me from living the life I wanted. This led me down the rabbit hole of making bad choices as the result of listening to influences I normally wouldn't.

But sometimes you want to be accepted and loved, and you stop caring where it comes from. If you find yourself in this place, it is time to lose the negative influences around you.

Are your relationships with these people meaningful, or are they filling a void of something you're lacking?

I have made many bad choices over the years. And each mistake can be linked back to choices I made to please others instead of listening to myself and trusting my gut. It's not that other people don't care about us or love us, but people usually have their own agendas in the front and center of their life—as they should.

Just don't let what THEY want become YOUR want, when you know that it's not true.

How do we do this?

LEARN HOW TO SAY NO and SET BOUND-ARIES!

You don't have to be a jerk about it. You can still be a loving human being who cares dearly for your friends and family. Just be careful not to become sucked up into their life and their drama. It's OK to say NO to a night out on the town when you just want to snuggle in with your family for a movie night.

I know what some of you are thinking: *I don't want to hurt their feelings. I don't want to upset anyone. I don't want them to think I don't care.*

That's fine and dandy, but my friends, you run this show. This is YOUR life—no one else's. So, take the time to do the things you want to do when you want to do them—even if it doesn't match someone else's plan for your life.

It has taken me a long time to get to the point where I can know and be okay with my decision. I now know that I am doing what is best for my family and me.

You are not responsible for how someone else reacts, as long as you weren't being an asshole. You have three responsibilities, as I learned from my friend, Heather Quisel:

1. Tell your truth in this life;

2. Live up to your word;

3. Do your best.

We have to acknowledge that we are all here for a reason. I truly believe we have a purpose and a gift to share. We just need to dig deep and figure out what amazing gifts we are holding back. These gifts will lead you to your truths. What are your values and beliefs?

If there's one thing in life we must stay strong and true to, it is our word. Do not promise things you cannot deliver, or agree to do something you can't guarantee.

Be true to your authentic self, or you will be miserable while doing it, which will simply attract negative experiences into your life.

Lastly, do your best. That's all any of us can do. No one is perfect, not even you. And why would you want to be? Honestly, how boring would your life be if you didn't have to put a little blood, sweat, and tears into your passion? Hard work just makes success that much sweeter.

We have to acknowledge that we are all here for a reason. I truly believe that we have a purpose and a gift to share, but we need to dig deep and figure out what amazing gifts we are holding back.

Learn to Delegate

When you have a million things on your plate, don't be afraid to ask for help. Don't be afraid to unload some of those commitments that are adding stress to your life if you are having trouble maintaining them.

Sometimes we need to take a step back and realize that we are not superwomen—no matter how hard we try. Stop doing the things that drag you down and steal your energy. Start looking for the things that motivate you and make you happy. Start following your dreams and taking the steps forward that you need to accomplish to make them happen.

Saying no does not make you a bad person. You need to know how much you can take on without making yourself crazy with worry and doubt, and letting negative thoughts creep in.

Steps to improve your life today

Here's a list of things you can do today to start living a life you can manage:

1. Start completing the mindful breathing exercises in chapter one. Not only will they help you start your day with a clear

head, but you can start on a positive note with that small happy feeling of living with your valve open.

2. Start reading books that can help you improve in the areas in which you are struggling. There so many self-help and development books that can help you become a better person and give you action steps to help you become the person you want to be. In the back of this book, you will find a list of all of the resources I have used to write this book. That's a good place to start. Don't be afraid to talk to others, or find groups online that have people in the same place you are who are trying to better themselves. Join our Battle Transformation group for continued support. Don't become stuck with people who are playing victim and are just looking for others to commiserate with instead of lifting each other up and moving forward.

3. Get rid of toxic people in your life. This can be hard, especially if the toxic people are family. This doesn't mean that they are bad people per se, but after spending time with them, you feel drained—as

though your energy has been sucked out of you. Probably because it has been. You know the people I'm talking about. You sit down and it becomes a major bitch session about everything wrong with their life, with no intention of changing it. They may try to suck you into their negative energy vortex and you will find you start to feel crabby and angry too. This is not what we are going for here. You don't have to call them out on it, but you don't have to feed in to their bitching. Just simply give them a one-word answer and move on to the next topic of conversation. If they don't lift you up or get you excited, they could be sucking up your positive energy and leaving you with their yuck. That's why you feel so crappy after seeing them.

They may belittle your ideas or fail to take you seriously. These are the people you do not need to spend time with. One thing we need to learn as we find ourselves and our backbone, is that you cannot—and do not have to—please everyone. That is one of those masks we wear.

One way to get rid of toxic people is to slowly wean them out of your day-to-day life. Now, sometimes you're stuck with a family member or co-worker. But you can keep yourself busy with your life and spend less time with them. It's OK to distance yourself and give yourself space to work on you. You don't need to be mean or hurt anyone's feelings because I know some of you are thinking *I'd feel bad*. Don't. You really don't have to. Remember, you are living your life for you now. Just start spending that time doing what you love. Remember, if you don't stand up for yourself, no one else is going to do it for you.

≡ suddenly ≡

you know...it's time

TO START SOMETHING NEW

and trust

the magic of beginnings.

Chapter 5: WHERE TO START?

So we want to change ourselves, but where are we going to find the time for that?

Are you kidding me? That's what I thought. Here is what my day looked like before I started trying to improve myself, because I knew there was something more I should be doing.

I thought to myself *extra time?* I have to drop kids off, go to work, kids have school, then hockey practice, home for baths, read books, bedtime, and crash on the couch with a glass of wine.

That's about where I was. Don't forget about watching the neighbors' kids on mornings "off" of work (which I truly enjoyed), then grocery shopping because your husband texted that he needed oatmeal and protein powder. Then you try to get to the Y for a quick workout. Take little P to 4K class, clean the house, work on your network marketing business, follow ups, reach outs, handle accounts. Shit! Time to leave to pick P up from 4K class.

You get the idea. I had no EXTRA time. Or so I thought.

What about that hour you could save combining all the separate 5-minute intervals of scrolling through Facebook? I'm all over here pushing the buttons: Like! Like! Ohhh, Love that! That's funny! Ha-ha! Ohhh, cute baby! PUPPIES! You get it! I knew I was wasting time and I was really starting to dislike that.

I started by reading. I read a lot of books and will provide a list of them on the resource page. They provided all my inspiration and ideas.

One book in particular helped changed things for me was Hal Elrods book, *Miracle Morning*—you should check it out!

The premise of the book is to change your morning routine so that you develop an amazing morning routine to start your day off with purpose, intention, and development. The best part is that the kids are usually still in bed, so this is time for you to focus on YOU! Enjoy, Momma!

Tips from Hal on getting your ASS out of bed!

1. Set your intentions the night before.

2. Keep your alarm clock across the room (this made me cringe a little bit!).

3. Brush your teeth.

4. Drink a full glass of water right when you wake up.

5. Get dressed.

Here are the steps that Hal outlines as a place to start each day ahead of the curve. He mentions six good habits that can be remembered by the acronym S.A.V.E.R.S

S—Silence—Meditation, Prayer, Reflection, Deep Breathing, Gratitude

We already talked about a lot of these! Do one or all—whatever works for you, but get out of bed to do it! Have a journal ready, your yoga DVD in, or find a recorded meditation. Now wake up and do it!

A—Affirmation—The most effective tool for becoming the person you need to be and achieve in life, is what you tell yourself about you. Affirmations are especially powerful when written out. They allow you to develop the mindset to take your life to the next level. Grab your pen and paper and get creative with what you want. Write down what you want every morning and what you are willing to do to get there.

V—Visualization—Make yourself comfortable in a quiet place. Close your eyes and start to imagine and picture your greatest desires and goals. What would completely change your life if you let it? Now, use all five of your senses to make your vision complete. What would it look, feel, smell, taste and sound like? Imagine yourself in the future accomplishing those goals. Actually see it in your mind and expect it to come.

E—Exercise—Yes, exercise again! Are you seeing a trend here? There is just too much science and proof that once you get your heart rate up and your blood is pumping, that your mind becomes clearer, you gain self-confidence, and you become ready for the day ahead. Even if it's a few jumping jacks or stretches, start there and see how much better equipped you are for your day.

R—Reading—Whatever your goals in life, someone is already an expert at it. This should not discourage you, but it should excite you! Someone else has learned how to do what you want to do. Why wouldn't you find that book and figure out how to do it too? There is so much knowledge, growth opportunities, and ideas out there on whatever we want to learn and become. Head to the library, Barnes & Noble, or Amazon. Start learning what you need to do to make your dreams come true.

S—Scribing—Write or journal about your thoughts and ideas. Take five to ten minutes to check in on your inner thoughts, insights, ideas, lessons learned, or areas in which you can improve or grow. It helps to find a journal that you love.

If you can implement these practices in your life every morning, I promise you, the growth you will see in yourself will blow your mind. You may even start to enjoy waking up early. That, my friend, is something I never thought I would say.

Don't forget to acknowledge the hard work you are doing. If there are parts of this process that you are not ready for, that is okay. Do what feels right now and come back to the other parts later. There is a lot of information in this book. Take note that it is not always easy. But then again nothing worth having comes easy!

life begins
at the end
—= OF YOUR =—
comfort zone!

Chapter 6: LIVING OUTSIDE YOUR COMFORT ZONE

We all have a space in our head that keeps us in check on our day-to-day actions. It is a safe place where we know we won't be challenged, questioned, or scared. We live in this place most of the time, because we feel secure with whom we are here.

If you have anxiety and depression, this is especially a safe place from the outside world where you can be easily overwhelmed. Things are the same in here and nothing changes. You know who you are and others know what to expect from you.

There is nothing wrong with being in your comfort zone. It is where we know who we are and it's familiar. The one thing you can't do here however is grow. You cannot flourish and produce new and exciting things in your life if you stay stuck in this place.

I'm not saying you can't come back to this space when you need to, but you have to try to venture out sometimes.

One of my favorite quotes hangs on my wall says, *Feel the fear, and do it anyway.*

Fear has had a bad rap. Fear is letting us know when we are on the verge of discovering something amazing within ourselves. It lets us know we are growing and reaching for better things in our life.

You have to trust that when you step outside of your comfort zone, you are really starting to live your life. The most exciting times in our lives happen outside our comfort zone; think about it.

The day you start your new job, go to a new restaurant, go back to school, take a chance on a network marketing business, get married, have children, buy a house... All of these things took place outside your comfort zone and they were the ones that we will always remember as special and important. You took a chance and let your true self come out to play. Think of how happy, emotional, and rewarding these events were. What if we lived in this place outside our comfort zone, knowing that at any time, we can go back to that cozy place?

Fear tells us that what we are about to do may be the greatest adventure worth taking. Of course, all of these decisions and experiences come with risk. You are going to fall and get bumps and bruises—this is normal. What do we tell our kids when this happens to them? *You're okay! You got this! Don't give up!*

We learn from our mistakes and can reconfigure as we go and see fit. If something doesn't work out, it doesn't mean it is wrong; it just means we need to pivot and go another direction. Nothing in our life happens to us, it happens for us and we need to start taking notice of what the universe is trying to tell us. We need to realize that we need to take a breath and enjoy the journey because if we don't, then WHY THE HELL ARE WE HERE?

We were made for so much more! It is time to start thinking about the things we want to do that are outside of our comfort zone. Those are the things we should be working towards and doing. Nothing amazing comes easy, and nothing easy is going to fulfill our true self and what we are made for.

Now, that's all fine and dandy you may think *But what if I have no idea what I want to do or what makes me tick or fires me up?* Let's take some time to dive into that and see if we can figure it out. Because you, my friend, are worth it.

What makes you special? What is it that you love to do what makes you happy and really gives you a glowing feeling inside that you feel from within?

It should feel like a warm giddiness that starts in the pit of your stomach and spreads throughout your body—this is what makes you special. It could be a hobby or just something that interests you.

What would you do if you had the day off all to yourself? Do you know what makes you interesting? What are you able to teach others? What do you do that you love? These are your gifts that you're meant to share. The things that make you excited or passionate just talking about it. Perhaps your friends come to you for advice on something. What can you teach and share in a place to help others?

Now keep in mind that this may put your ego at risk. *What the hell does that mean*? It means that when you step outside your comfort zone, you're going to feel uncomfortable and weird. You're going to feel as though you have no idea what you're doing, and that's ok.

It's your EGO's job to make you feel this way. Your ego is your conscious mind and its job is to keep you safe, but in doing so can cause a lot of misery and lost time.

One thing our ego is good at, is comparing ourselves to others. This is such a waste of time. All we are going to do by comparing ourselves to someone else is to feel tired, unproductive and start the whole cycle of negative thoughts ruminating in our heads.

Most of the time you won't even realize you are doing this until you have spent too long stewing over someone else's success when you could be celebrating with them. Everyone feels envy at times, and we compare ourselves to others. Unfortunately, this doesn't serve us even a little bit.

When you start to appreciate other people's successes instead of tearing them down, you will find that success will come your way quicker and easier. When you let go of jealousy, you can live more productively, with your own thoughts and ideas, and you can create the life YOU love.

Here are some ideas from Jenn Carrington on mantras you can use throughout the day to keep your mind in check.

Someone else's success never takes away from my own.

I am not in competition with (insert the names of people you compare yourself with).

It is not my place to question someone else's success and whether or not they deserved it.

I have my own stories to share, work to do, and contribution to bring to the world—even if others are also doing something similar.

Look at these and feel the power behind them.

Exercises from Jenn Carrington

While you're doing this, take out your journal. Take a moment to answer these questions.

1. Jot down all of the things that are causing you jealousy right now. Dive even deeper into that envy and explore—what am I jealous of? Do I even want what they have? What can this jealousy teach me about my core desires right now?

2. Be bigger than your envy—are there any friends and peers whose recent success you haven't celebrated because jealousy got in the

way? Be brave enough to reach out and cheer them on. Are there any projects you've been afraid to work on because you've compared yourself to others who are already doing something similar? Get started anyway and believe that there's enough space for you all.

Your ego doesn't care what dreams you have or what you really want to do. Your ego just wants you to be safe but it can stop you from reaching your true potential. It wants to keep you safe, which is helpful, but it should not always be in control of your life.

For most of us, our ego runs our life and is ruining it. It may even be preventing us from putting our thoughts and feelings out there for the world to see.

My ego nearly prevented me from writing this book! Seriously! While writing this book, my ego told me daily that it was a bad idea and no one would read it. Guess what? I wrote it anyway! It didn't even kill me to do it. A few times, I thought it might, but alas, I am still here!

Risking your ego means that you may be embarrassed, self-conscious, and you may make others uncomfortable. The human ego loves external admiration and validation. But we can let go of ego so we can do what we need to do to, which is to step out of our comfort zones and to live a life we love.

We can never get rid of the ego completely, but we can learn to grow and take chances without the ego driving our decisions. Although the ego has a purpose, left uncheck it can prevent us from living in attachment to our higher self.

If you're feeling anxious, worried, overwhelmed, impatient, stressed, or experience emotional discomfort, you are living within your ego and it makes you feel mistreated and defensive. You are only focused on yourself and your survival.

Is Ego Running Your Life?

You can quickly establish whether your ego is controlling your life by honestly pondering the following traits.

You have a need for control. The ego thinks that uncertainty equals danger and therefore, it wants you to control everything so that it doesn't end up hurt.

You have to be right. You may have a hard time admitting when you're wrong and others are right. Ego thinks everything is judged good or bad, right or wrong—there's no gray space in the middle. Unfortunately, this kind of thinking can lead to judging and criticizing others. It also prevents our creative side moving forward and enjoying positive teamwork.

You feel like you can't have fun. Everything is serious. Ego feeds from our negative thoughts and is always on the lookout for things that may hurt us, even if it's not a reality. It can steal pleasure by replacing it with worry, concern, guilt, shame, and humiliation. It makes up this horribly negative story that it wants to tell us again and again until we start believing it.

Ego must always win. This is different to healthy competition. It will distract you from the real important things in life, such as personal growth and development. It will prevent you from helping others learn. It doesn't enjoy mutual growth or making meaningful connections.

The need to be perfect. Ego makes us think that unless everything is perfect, we are not good enough, or not worthy. This need to be perfect is a way to show the world that we can handle it all, even if we are full of anxiety and dread on the inside. Perfectionism tends to stall us. It prevents us from spending time with our families or enjoying doing so, because we are too focused on how we look or what our house looks like. What would happen if someone came over and saw my house a mess? What would that say about me? Maybe that I am incompetent or incapable. Obviously, these thoughts couldn't be further from the truth. I catch myself saying them to myself all the time. *Come on over, but don't mind the mess.* Or *my house is a disaster*. Really, who cares? Not anyone that matters.

Take some time and ask yourself what else could you spend time doing if you didn't have to be perfect all time? Whom could you spend time with? What could you do? How much more time would you have to enjoy yourself?

* * *

So how do we kick egos ass?

Or at least, prevent it from controlling your life all of the time?

If you can follow your heart and live out of your love and your purpose, you will know. It will be easy, because it's what you're good at and what you enjoy doing. It is easy to be courageous in the face of fear. You'll have everything you need and it will be easier to tell ego to take a spot in the backseat.

Perhaps the most important thing we can do is to live in the here and now. Live for the moment.

When we are living in the past, we become depressed. We have ruminating thoughts that we think repeatedly. These are things that have already happened and we cannot change. They make us feel sad and lonely.

Ego loves to replay these tapes in our heads, and it's time for us to turn them off. We all make mistakes; they happen and we need to learn from them and move on. Mistakes are part of the journey: there is no one on earth who has not experienced this.

It's OK when things are not perfect. That is when we learn and make ourselves better people. The only problem is when we can't move on and we stay in this place of negativity.

If you suffer from anxiety, you're most likely living in the future. Ego hates uncertainty and the unknown. When we are unable to predict the future, it makes us feel uncomfortable, uneasy, and anxious.

Too much is never enough. We constantly feel like we need to acquire more and more for the fear of lacking or not having enough. This served the hunters and gatherers well back in their time, but in this world of instant gratification, we have everything that we need, however, we continue to acquire to appease the ego. The best thing we can do is reign in our impulse buys and acquisitions. We should try to show gratitude for what we have and enjoy the people around us, instead of our things.

As you start on this journey to improve yourself, there will always be critics. The ego is going to want to self-preserve. Don't let it. Continue to live out of happiness and in doing so, add value. How you choose to live your life does not concern anyone else! Your friends may see you changing and this is going to make them uncomfortable. It's time for you to decide who you want to be and where you want to go.

worrying

DOESN'T TAKE AWAY
TOMORROW'S TROUBLES.

it takes away today's peace.

Chapter 7: **EVOLVE**

I don't know if you have noticed, but the idea of mindset is really starting to catch on. People are realizing that if you get your mind right, the rest will follow. Now naturally, as someone who suffers from anxiety and depression, we could use some getting our head right.

Once we look at what is really going on in our heads, it can be a bit shocking to find how unkind we are to ourselves.

We need to start treating ourselves as we treat our best friends. If we can figure out the mindset game, we will have it made it, I kid you not.

We cannot depend on the world to change for us, so we have to articulate and know what we want from the world. The things you think about daily have such an impact on what happens in our life.

You can choose what you want your life to look like by changing your thoughts. Think about all the uber-successful people in the world. They all practice the mindset game.

* * *

The first thing we need to do is to pay attention to your thoughts and what you tell yourself every day.

We all have this continued mind stream that has thoughts constantly running through it. To be exact, you can have up to 60,000 thoughts in a day and science has shown that for many people, most of those thoughts are negative. That should get your attention!

The good news is that you can learn to change the type of thoughts you want to have and get rid of the ones we don't want. When we start to do this practice every day, we will be on our way to a happier self.

In 2005, the National Science Foundation published an article after researching how many thoughts humans have per day. The average person has about 12,000 to 60,000 thoughts per day. Of those, 80% are negative. Of those 80% negative thoughts, 95% are exactly the same repetitive thoughts as the day before. Data from: Wayne E. Evans, Ph.D.

Our thoughts have a direct correlation with our health. This can cause high blood pressure, migraines, body aches, ulcers, and an overall feeling of "blah". Blah is probably not the scientific name for the emotion, but you know that feeling. You just don't feel right and can't put your finger on what it is.

The problem is that we run on low vibrational emotions, which don't connect with our true self.

I believe that "blah" feeling is when our thoughts, feelings, and emotions have led us down that slippery slope of negative thinking that directly impacts our bodies. For the sake of our health and wellness, we have to look at fixing our mindset. Mindset is everything, my friend. When you can get your mindset in check, your life will begin to improve dramatically.

Imagine all the thoughts you have in a day floating down a stream. Then, imagine getting rid of the thoughts you don't want to experience repeatedly. You must do the work to get there, though. You can't just read the book. Get your journal out and follow along!

Thought-Stream Exercise

Would you like to see what your mind stream looks like?

Find a quiet and comfortable place after your kids or spouse are sleeping or when you're alone at home. You won't get much out of this when you are wondering if they are starting the house on fire while you take a minute to yourself. Trust me it will be worth it.

You will need a notebook and pen. Get comfortable, and turn off all distractions. Yes, even your phone. Gasp!

So now that you have your spot and your distractions are gone, let's take a moment to see what is going on in your head. This can be a little scary and uncomfortable at first, but it gets better, I promise.

You are going to sit for 3-5 minutes in this quiet place. Just sit. Your mind will wander, which is normal.

Start to take some deep breaths. Focus on the air going in your nose down to your lungs and out your mouth. Put your hand on your chest to help you feel the breaths.

Now, start to focus on the thoughts you are having. It could just be words or sentences. It may even be things you see in the room around you—whatever you need to get started.

You will start to notice your true thoughts shift to the forefront of your mind. Start writing them down.

There is no right or wrong way to do this, so just write down everything that pops in to your head. Do this for at least twenty minutes. Take more time if you have thoughts left after the twenty minutes are up. When you feel as though you have captured your thoughts, stop.

Look at your paper. This is a snippet of what is going on in your head when you are not paying attention or tending to your thoughts.

What are you focusing on? Is it positive or negative? We are often surprised to learn that most of our ruminating thoughts are negative. Don't be alarmed, because this is normal. But now that you are aware of it, you can change it by cultivating your mind.

Think of your thoughts as a stream or a garden. Your mind and thoughts are a garden that has been abandoned and has become overgrown and wild. As you become more aware of your thoughts, you can begin to pick the weeds (negative thoughts) out and get rid of them by acknowledging that they are there but that they are untrue and made up by the ego. You can then plant new ideas and thoughts that you can cultivate and nurture to get your garden back under control.

As you work on this and practice mindfulness, you will find the weeds keep popping up. Acknowledge them and their falseness. You will become much better at knowing what those weeds and negative thoughts are and better equipped to pull them out and replace them with a positive thought quicker and with less work.

Sometimes, the negative thoughts can be stubborn, and even after you pull the weeds, you might need to get the weed killer and imagine spraying some of that on those thoughts too. You will have to check your stream or garden almost daily to keep yourself in check. Over time though, this gets easier and you can call a negative thought out right away and tell it to get the hell out of your garden.

You can also imagine a stream and watch your thoughts float by on a leaf. Sometimes, if you just acknowledge the thoughts and let them float by without reacting to them it makes it easier to let them go.

After looking at your thoughts, you may begin to see the negative patterns that have formed in your brain.

What can you do to change your thoughts and begin to have a more positive mindset?

First, think about how you feel when you are feeling these negative thoughts; they make you feel bad. Some examples may be stress, concern, frustration, worry, doubt, guilt, sadness, anger, loneliness, rage, resentment.

These thoughts clearly make us feel low, we then vibrate at a lower frequency and we tend to stuff them down where we don't have to deal with them. When we do that, they start to fester and grow and wreak havoc on the inside. Usually, they are unleashed on some poor, unsuspecting soul who was just trying to talk to us.

Have you ever gone off on someone for no reason and right after felt like crap? Yeah, that's what happens when those negative thoughts come out. We start to become defensive and asshole-ish— no fun to be around! So, make sure you take the time to acknowledge and replace those negative thoughts.

When the negative thoughts start kicking in tell them they are not wanted and replace them with a positive thought of any kind. Find anything else to focus your mind on. When you are truly present in a moment you can focus your thoughts on anything in the here and now using your five senses.

How to Manifest What You Want in This Life

What if you could change your mindset and negate the results of all of your negative thinking?

Good news: you can do that at any time. The easiest way to do this is to SMILE. That's right; all you need to do to start feeling good is smile.

When you smile, close your eyes, feel it coming from deep inside you. It's not just any smile, though; it is the smile you have when one of your kids gives you the biggest, sweetest hug or when your cat curls up on your lap. It's the smile you may have when you see a box full of puppies in front of you. It's the smile you have when you accomplish something for which you have been working so hard.

Get creative! That smile will start a small, warm buzz inside of you. You have to be open to the feeling deep in your soul. It will start as a tiny shift in your energy as you open up your heart to an instant feel good vibration. Everything is made up of energy so when you do this you get your energy running at a higher frequency. This high frequency is then sent out to the world. Because high frequencies attract other high frequencies (law of attraction), you can start to declare your wants to the universe, and they will begin to show up in your life. You get what you put out to the universe. Like a boomerang—what you put out comes back to you.

In the book *Excuse me! Your life is waiting*, Lynne Grabhorn explains that nothing is more important than feeling good. She provides the steps to take for that inner, warm smile to open yourself and allow the universe to bring you your wants and desires.

I think about it like a lever or valve inside us. When we are in a feel-good state and our vibrations are running high, our "inner valves" are open, and what we want will come to us. You need to figure out what you want and how to state it as a positive intent, so you don't get more of what you don't want. You need to state your wants to the universe from the place of what it would feel like to have that want rather than the lack of having your want. I know that may sound confusing. So here are the steps to getting what you want in life!

Steps to Manifesting Your Wants

1. Find what you DON'T want. Easy! Example *"I don't want to pay rent anymore."*

2. Turn that in to what you DO want. Write it out as a positive want. "I want my own home!" See how that comes from a place of want rather than don't want. Write your WANTS down! Get creative and don't play small!

3. Get in the feeling place of that want. Start thinking about the details of your want! What does it look, feel, smell or sound like? Envision every detail of the house.

4. Expect, listen, and allow it to happen. You have to let the universe know that you anticipate your want to come to you!

If you want a new house, describe how it would look. Where is it located? What does the yard look like? How it would be decorated, the paint colors, how much it would cost, how amazing it feels to sit in your living room... Keep thinking about it until you can actually picture this house in your mind. Bring yourself to this happy, warm image of the house.

Writing things down is so powerful. It may help you to figure out the specifics of your want. Once you have your want established, you have that warm buzz in the pit of your stomach from your smile, you can begin writing all of the details of your want. You need to EXPECT it is coming. LISTEN and WATCH for it, and ALLOW it to happen.

Focus on what you want with excitement and passion and let it come to you. Remember, it is our FEELINGS that create the vibrations that are sent out. The universe will send back vibrations on the same magnitude.

We have to find a way to feel good about our wants. Rather than longing, wishing, or needing it—those all come from fear, and negative feelings that lead us to more low vibrations. That brings us more of what we DON'T want.

As long as you don't focus on the fact that you don't have it and you have no idea how you will obtain it, it will come. You do not have to figure out how to make it happen!

A great exercise to feel joyful about your want is to ask yourself: *WHY?* This question is a fantastic jumpstart for your want. So, let's take the house example. You know you want a new house.

Why? Come up with every reason why you want to own your home.

I could decorate it however I want!

I want a yard for my kids to play in!

If you are coming up with what you DON'T want, you have to change it to what you DO want. "Don't wants" come from negative energy, so you need to flip them into coming from a place of wanting. Do that by answering with the word BECAUSE...

- *Because I would feel safe and secure.*

- *Because I want my kids to be able to run around and explore.*

- *Because I want to grow a beautiful garden.*

Start imagining that house inside and out.

If you can stay in this mindset for 16 seconds, you are bringing those things your way. The more you do this and the longer you stay in that place of bliss with your valve open, the faster your want will come to you. Once you have become good at coming up with your wants, start to intend that they will come.

Intending is combining **I expect** and **I want,** which creates new pathways for us to send our energy, instead of on the negative thoughts that we ruminate in our mind daily. The next step is to get a little creative with our wants. We have lived in this comfort zone of ease for so long that we forgot what it is like to dream and think BIG.

Start with the ***want***.

I want to own property, then add the *because I want a place to call my own*—intend it to be true—and *I intend to bring it to life*.

I intend to have the house of my dreams. I intend to have the money to pay the mortgage. I intend to find a job I love to pay for the house.

Then you need to stop and listen, pay attention, and allow your wants to come.

You need to start listening to that little voice in your head. You know when that little crazy idea pops into your head that you think would be awesome, but you dismiss it because it seems too crazy or unattainable. You are saying no to inner self, which is like saying *I don't want to be happy or excited. I want to play safe and live how I am now.*

IF you are okay with that, good for you! But if you are reading this book, I'm guessing you are looking for something more in your life. Start listening and paying attention to what the universe is trying to send your way. Start thinking about what you can do instead of thinking, *Yeah, but...* excuse, excuse, excuse.

* * *

If we are all Debbie-downers feeling sorry for ourselves, we will attract more of the same. More of the same circumstances, emotions, interactions. It is time to use a little tough love here.

You have to get up and get moving. I don't care where you go or what you do, but GET UP AND MOVE!

The longer we stay in bed wishing things were different, the more of the same we will get. We need to realize no one is going to do this for us. We need to change our lives for US!

YOU ARE WORTH IT! You deserve to have a life you love and cherish. You were not sent to this world to live a so-so life with mediocre circumstances feeling sorry for yourself. You must change the way your brain is functioning. I know this is not always easy, especially if you are in some major depression. But I had to learn to stop using that as my crutch and excuse for not doing what I wanted in life, and so can you.

If you are still struggling. See a doctor, wait the two weeks for a medication to start kicking in, and see if you can get your meds adjusted if you need to after that. Come back to this book when you are ready.

You should also know it is NOT selfish to have a great life. We should all be able to live the life that makes us excited and happy and in return sends out more fast and high vibrations to bring us more of what we want.

DON'T CRY OVER THE PAST, IT'S GONE.

don't stress about the future.

it hasn't arrived.

live in

the present and make it beautiful.

Chapter 8: THE BATTLE

As you work your way through this book, you may find yourself totally all in at first. You feel ready to change your life, things are looking up, and everything is going great.

Soon enough, negative things start happening. The washer breaks, the kids are sick, the dog puked all over your white rug (true story). It all just seems like too much.

You decide it's too hard and you quit trying to better yourself. Let me tell you, this is not your fault. Whenever we start to improve ourselves and work to get ahead in life, we will be tested. There will be a mental war, and the universe will ask you how badly you really want it. It will be up to you if you want to battle on and win, or give up and stay stuck where you are.

There will be times when it feels like there are forces out of your control that are holding you back. It may feel like everyone is against you or that the world does not want you to succeed.

If you can identify when this is happening and call it out, you are going to win. Recognize that the resistance means that you are just on the other side of changing your life. You just need to stick to your battle plan a little longer, and put a little more work and energy in. Don't quit and you will come out on the other side the victor of the battle.

The battle may feel like fear, doubt, criticism, and procrastination. It is not rational and will make you feel uncomfortable. Take note that this means you are soooo close to living in sync with your higher self. This is the time to dig in your heels and know that your accomplishments are within your reach. It is easy to get overwhelmed on this journey. Learn to use your mistakes as a part of the process and use them to grow and make yourself stronger. Others may project their doubt, fear, and skepticisms on to us. Do not quit fighting!

Most people will quit with the finish line within their reach! They just don't see it because there may be a hill in the way and people are trying to pull you back down. But once you get to the top, you will see your goal is just a bit further. You may trip, stumble, and fall down; in fact, this should be expected in life!

You just need to focus on your direction and your purpose. Pick yourself up and keep going, because when you are victorious, it will all be worth it. Don't let those who are watching life happen to them impact, influence, and dictate how you battle. For they have never even tried; why would they deserve to critique your battle plan?

The battle will feed on fear and show up as rejection. People may try to make you feel bad and become angry because you are changing. This is not your concern. You need to stop the opposing forces by doing what you feel is right. Know that you are strong enough, smart enough, and armed with the tools you need to be successful on this journey.

Chapter 9: WHEN THE SEASONS MESS WITH OUR BATTLE

I'll be damned if you won't be feeling amazing and then—bam!—the next thing you know you are back to square one. You will be asking yourself *what the heck just happened. I was feeling so good!*

We need to start being aware of how we are feeling during the seasons and how the sun and light can impact how we feel. We need to remember that if we are prone to depression, that the season can greatly impact how we feel.

It's officially known as Seasonal Affective Disorder. The farther away you get from the equator the higher the prevalence, as there is less daylight in the winter months. If you know that you suffer from S.A.D. and you are already taking medications for anxiety and depression, you may need to increase your dosage or add a medication. Speak to your doctor about this.

So, if we weren't feeling sorry for ourselves already, we now add to that the middle of January. When the sun comes out for an hour or two if we are lucky, we find ourselves holed up in our houses, waiting for spring. After twenty years, I have figured out that if I don't increase my anti-depressant in November, I am a hot mess by the end of December. Then, if you add the stress of the holidays and all the events and parties, things can escalate pretty quickly. The worst part is that I KNOW this about myself and I always think I'm going to be OK. Maybe this will be the year I won't need to increase my dose. Then I find myself upset or crying over something I would never normally be upset about, and know that I missed my transition period. That means I have to play catch up with my medication.

Usually, if you have a physician you have developed a relationship with, you can talk to them about your S.A.D. and about increasing your dose if you do worse in the winter months. Always be sure to check with your physician before making any changes.

Supplements can also help keep your depression and anxiety in check. Here's a list of things I have found to help keep depression and S.A.D. in check:

Vitamin D

If you have never had your vitamin D level checked, start there. Again, talk with your physician and they can order a simple lab to see if you lack vitamin D. I found that I was severely low and once I added Vitamin D to my daily routine, I could actually notice a difference. Usually, vitamin D is sold in 1,000-2,000 IUs. You can buy it over the counter.

Fish Oil

The next supplement to consider would be fish oil. Fish oil supplements may help ease symptoms of depression in some people. Some studies in adults suggest that omega-3 fatty acids may be beneficial in the treatment of mild to moderate depression, but more research is needed, according to Mayo Clinic.

Fish oil is a good source of omega-3 fatty acids, which play an important role in brain function. People with depression may have low blood levels of brain chemicals that we are aware of that can be found in fish oil. Fish oil also can be purchased easily over the counter and is good for your heart, so there's a win-win.

Exercise

You knew this one was coming!

Get outside and exercise. If you live somewhere cold, you need to find something you enjoy doing outside and then learn how to dress warm. Layers, layers, layers!

The last thing any of us with anxiety and depression should be doing is lying in a dark room with no sunlight, waiting to feel better. Because IT'S NOT GOING TO HAPPEN BY ITSELF.

You have to want to get better. Now, I am not suggesting that any of us like feeling this way. But I do think at some point—if we are not doing the things we need to do to get better—we are being lazy and a bit selfish; especially to those around us who love us and who deserve for us to show up and be our best self.

It's hard, I know. Trust me, you can get there. You must TAKE ACTION.

I don't care what you do but get up and move your body. The research on benefits of exercise on mood is just overwhelming. You don't need to run a marathon, but you do have to move.

Light Therapy

Spend your money on a fancy S.A.D. light. They have special bulbs that can give you the replicated affects you get from natural sunlight.

When the seasons are changing and the days start to become shorter, there can be a chemical imbalance. Our circadian rhythm changes and that can really mess with us.

Light therapy is as simple as just using the light for an hour or two a day. S.A.D. lights have been proven to improve moods. You could have it by your computer while you work or beside you while you watch TV. I have seen some improvement with this and it's easy, so it may be worth trying.

One thing that has helped me as well has been going to a tanning bed (shh) a couple of times during the winter. I'm not condoning the use of tanning beds, as we all know that they can cause skin cancer, but there is something about getting those rays that helps lift my mood. This is not something I do often, but it can help me get out of a funk.

Stop APOLOGIZING!

We do this all the time even when we have no need to apologize for anything. I don't know where or why I started doing this but I apologize for things that I have no control over, or things that don't have anything to do with me.

Not only is this another way to feel like you did something wrong, but it makes you think you actually did something "bad" in the first place. When you catch yourself apologizing for something you had no part of, change your words.

If you are trying to be empathetic—instead of saying "I'm sorry"—acknowledge the issue at hand. For example, instead of "I'm sorry you had a bad day", try "That must be (frustrating, aggravating, maddening, sad, etc.)". When you apologize because you were raised to think it is polite, remember that it runs a negative circuit in your brain, which makes you feel worse. Ask yourself, why am I apologizing? Most of the time it is probably unwarranted.

Say NO. This goes hand in hand with the apologizing. Start putting your needs before everyone else's. It's kind of like the oxygen mask in the airplane. Don't overbook or stress yourself out if it's not something for which you have the time and energy.

It's okay to be selfish with your time! People will go above and beyond at work or take on too many things, causing them to end up frazzled and stressed out. Then when you come home, you are crabby and short with the ones you love the most. It's not fair to our spouses or kids. Being kind and helpful is great, but not at the expense of those you love.

I know it's hard, but the worst thing in the world we can do is to play the victim and poor me syndrome. Take things easy until you are feeling a little better, but don't stop living because you are going to feel worse. Call a friend, talk it out, cry, and get back on the horse. Life is too precious to waste being sad.

Let's talk about crying for a second. I used to think that not crying was a sign that I was tough and strong, but as I have figured out who I am, I have realized that my thinking was so wrong.

Crying gets a bad rap, but it helps us relieve stress and is good for our mental health. So go ahead have a sob fest. Feel the release of all of the anxiety.

If you are looking for permission, I am giving it to you now. If we can give ourselves those moments and feel those emotions, we can acknowledge how we feel and move on without feeling as if we are adding more baggage. Feel the feelings and move on!

If you can take what you have learned in this book, and couple that with the exercises you are going to find, you will be on your way to living a life you love even when times are tough.

* * *

There are many ways we can deal with S.A.D., but perhaps the best thing we can do is to know it is coming, especially if it happens every year. Know that you have the tools to deal with this and it does not need to control you or your life.

Chapter 10: THE DAY-TO-DAY

A great way to declutter your mind is to declutter your house! One thing you can do to help the mind calm is to keep the space around you tidy and uncluttered. There is a great book out there called "The Life-Changing Magic of Tidying Up". I would highly recommend reading it for the complete process.

Go through each room of your home. Get rid of any extra papers, junk and clutter that do not evoke a feeling of happiness and joy. A great place to start is your closet. Take all your clothes out and go through one by one. When you hold the article of clothing in your hands decide if it makes you happy and makes you feel good. If you are not sure or think you might need it some day. Donate it! Do this for all articles of clothing in your closet and dressers. Continue this process for every room in your house. Get rid of anything you don't need that doesn't speak positively to you.

Once you have decluttered you can move on to organizing. Come up with a centralized place for papers and go out and buy some cute organizational shelves, boxes or baskets for your miscellaneous things you have. Give everything a home location and return it there after each use. This has helped me keep our house somewhat put together. This is great for kids to get rid of their extra toys too. Make them part of the process!

* * *

Another thing that can help during the day to day. Take a moment to chill the *BLEEP* out.

We are so tightly wound that we can't even have a conversation with those close to us. Have you ever asked someone how he or she is? What do you say when someone asks you? The answer is ALWAYS, *"Oh, I've been busy. Busy, busy, busy."*

Now don't get me wrong. I love to get my hands in many things and I like it that way. But when did we become so preoccupied with our lives that we can't sit down and have a normal conversation with someone, that is a problem.

Instead, we rely on text or short messages to pass on information and relay how we are feeling. It's all a little bit cold and sad if you ask me.

I'm not saying busy is bad because I love being busy. But are you busy with the right things? Can you stop and take a break and breathe without feeling as if your whole world is going to come crumbling down? I know the schedule: work, school, kids' sports, dinner, family time, activities, and life gets to be a lot.

Did you even eat anything healthy today or just on the go snacks?

Be careful that you are not just going through the motions. If you are, it is time to change something. We were not sent here to be miserable and we are not meant to not have time for fun and adventures. TRUST ME.

If you are unhappy with your job, find something you ENJOY doing. When you enjoy your work, it's not work. Don't tell me you can't find a job. I know you have to be realistic about your income and paying your bills, but have you ever looked at what you really want to be doing and considered it actually could be a reality?

If you don't believe that you deserve that, then we need to work on your self-confidence. There is plenty of time on this earth to find what works for you. We are never stuck or permanently forced to do a job unless we make it that way. You could walk out and leave at any time.

Now, it would obviously be best to do this with a realistic back up plan. Give it some thought:

- What do you love?

- What speaks to you?

- What could you spend the rest of your life doing?

- What do you need to do to make that dream a reality?

This is where you need to start. It can be yours, friend. You just have to believe in yourself and take action. Get ready, because we are going to do that right now.

* * *

The next exercise is going to help you come up with three goals you are going to focus on for ONE year!

Open your mind, get your creative juices flowing, and let's change your life! Find me on www.lauramausolf.com for some accountability.

Doing this exercise, introduced to me by Heather Quisel, changed my life. This helped me grow and evolve. One thing I did was write this book. This was something I never thought I had the confidence or ability to do. What can it do for you?

For real, are you ready? Change Your Life Exercise

CHANGING YOUR LIFE STARTS NOW!

Come up with 100 THINGS you want to ACHIEVE, SEE, ACCOMPLISH, DO OR ACQUIRE. Write them down.

As you finish your 100 things bucket list, you may find that you have stifled your creative mind for what you are "supposed" to be doing or how you are supposed to fit into society. What if you left your old, negative thoughts behind and believed that you deserve and should have these things?

* * *

HINTS for a successful list: Nothing is off limits. Money is not an object. Think BIG. This is not a TO DO list. It may take you a while to come up with 100 things, because we suck at thinking up stuff we deserve. Write down all those big and amazing things. What have you always wanted to

do or see or have? Where would you love to go?
HAVE FUN WITH THIS!

THINGS

1.	34.	67.
2.	35.	68.
3.	36.	69.
4.	37.	70.
5.	38.	71.
6.	39.	72.
7.	40.	73.
8.	41.	74.
9.	42.	75.
10.	43.	76.
11.	44.	77.
12.	45.	78.
13.	46.	79.

14.	47.	80.
15.	48.	81.
16.	49.	82.
17.	50.	83.
18.	51.	84.
19.	52.	85.
20.	53.	86.
21.	54.	87.
22.	55.	88.
23.	56.	89.
24.	57.	90.
25.	58.	91.
26.	59.	92.
27.	60.	93.
28.	61.	94.
29.	62.	95.
30.	63.	96.

31.	64.	97.
32.	65.	98.
33.	66.	99.
		100.

CONGRATULATIONS!

This is actually a very difficult exercise! I was introduced to this by my mentor, Heather Quisel. When I did this my first goal was to write this book! It works, trust me. Dream big.

It is hard for people who are always taking care of others to stop and ask themselves what they want. I want you to know that it's not selfish or egotistical; it is your right as a human on this planet to do things that inspire you and make you happy. Put the millions of hats you wear everyday out of your mind, and focus on just you for a moment. Yes, while you are feeding your baby and your other kids are fighting.

Now that doesn't mean we can't want things for our family and children, but that's not what we are working on. We are making you better and stronger for them. The goal is to return your purpose and put the spark back in your life.

Take a minute to read over your 100 Things List and imagine what it would be like to have any number of those things in your life right now. Guess what? You can! No, I am not full of shit.

Here is what we are going to do. Take those 100 things and circle your Top 10 things that you want to accomplish. They should make you feel excited and nervous—maybe even a little scared. If it scares you that is definitely a sign you should do it. That just means they are what you should be doing. Keep in mind at this time that you don't have to know how you are going to accomplish these things, or how you are going to bring them to you. You don't need to worry about that right now. I want you to pick something that puts a smile on your face and gives you that warm, excited, buzzed-up feeling we were talking about when we were manifesting things in to our lives.

* * *

How do you pick?

Let's look at how we can narrow down your list and get to the good stuff.

First, cross off all of your TO DO list items. Things like finishing the basement, cleaning the closet, organizing the kids' clothes. Cross those babies off!

Next, cross off the feelings. Things such as I want to be happy, confident, smarter, more successful. Those get the axe too.

Now, look at what you have left. What sticks out to you? What is something you have always wanted to do but you have let fear talk you out of it? What if you left your baggage and masks aside and changed your mindset to believe that you were meant for more?

Look at your list now and narrow it down to your top 10. This should take some time and reflective thought. Don't try to rush through this exercise. When you are ready, I want you to come up with your Top 3 Goals for the next 365 days. It doesn't matter when you are starting. Mark the one-year date in your calendar.

You do not need to know how it's going to happen, or if it will work... That's not up to you. The only truth we know is that if we don't try, we will never know. Your top three should scare and excite you at the same time. We are going to plan the path here and now. You might get lost or off course and that's OK. Use your goals as a compass to change the course and get back on track.

There is no guarantee, but if you practice the things you have learned in this book, I promise you will bring big things your way this year. The universe will always give us what we need; we just have to be open to receiving it and be willing to trust the truths we are being sent.

Take those three goals and follow along as we to draw "our map" to where we want to be.

This is an awesome time in your life. Everything can change if you let it. Have faith and trust that the journey will be exactly what it needs to be and you will get what you need when you are ready.

Top 3 Goals

1.

2.

3.

Congratulations! You have your top three goals! Now how are we going to make these goals happen?

I want you to fill out a page for each goal. You are going to figure out what resources you need to fulfill that goal and then what action steps you need to make for this to happen.

GOAL # 1:_____

Resources Needed to Complete Goal From Start to
Finish:

<u>Action Steps Needed to Take to Accomplish Goal:</u>

GOAL # 2:_____

Resources Needed to Complete Goal From Start to Finish:

Action Steps Needed to Take to Accomplish Goal:

GOAL # 3:_____

<u>Resources Needed to Complete Goal From Start to Finish:</u>

Action Steps Needed to Take to Accomplish Goal:

You now have a plan of attack to tackle your top three goals for the next year. How amazing is that? This is the beginning of living for you and finding whom you really are. Write your top three down and post them where you can see them! You can find YOU again underneath all the baggage of your past, masks to hide the real you, and day-to-day mom life. You owe it to yourself and your family to try.

Make sure you tell them what you are doing and why, especially if it interferes with the time they usually spend with you. Be sure to tell them what it MEANS to you and how it can help your family going forward. Can your family do anything to help you reach your goals? Imagine how cool would your kids think it would be to help you transform your life!

This is where your morning routine can be greatly beneficial. Getting the extra work done before anyone else is awake is an amazing way to get where you want to go without impacting what you currently are doing. For busy people with full plates, this is where you FIND the TIME. Plus, it gives you time to focus on YOU.

The Battle is something we all go through at some point in our lives, whether we are just going through a bad time in our lives or want to find happiness, and we just can't figure out how. The steps you have taken just by reading this book and doing the exercises will lead you to great and amazing things you never knew you were capable of. Your job as a parent can be stressful, crazy, and your greatest challenge. It will also be what we are most proud and thankful for.

When we begin this journey to find ourselves, our families will notice. They will notice the way you hold your head a little higher, you back a little straighter, and speak more confidently. Feel good about your growth and decide what you need to do from here on out to keep what you have learned fresh in your mind.

What will be your first step to execute your first life goal? You got this—you always had it—you just needed to be cheered on. I am here to tell you that you are worth it and you can do this.

The battle is never completely over, but we are winning and our children are watching us, learning, and taking it all in. Be proud of yourself and know that they have an amazing mother. Anxiety and depression do not define you. It will not stop you from being who you are meant to be. Your life is starting a new right now, from this moment forward. I can't wait to see where you go!

* * *

For continued support in your life and on this journey come and join us at The Battle Transformation group! Find it on my website www.lauramausolf.com. I will be there to help, encourage and cheer you on. If you want a coach along the way I would be glad to help you through this process. You got this!

RESOURCES

Burg, Bob, and John David Mann. The go-Giver: a little story about a powerful business idea. Portfolio/Penguin, 2015.

Carnegie, Dale, and Fakhroll Rodziee Don. How to stop worrying and start living. PTS Professional Publishing, 2013.

Carnegie, Dale. How to win friends and influence people. HarperCollins Publishers Australia, 2017.

Cloud, Henry, et al. Boundaries. Zondervan, 2001.

Cloud, Henry, and John Sims Townsend. Boundaries. Zondervan, 2004.

"Eight Mantras & Reminders For When You're Feeling Anxious & Overwhelmed In Your Business." Jen Carrington, www.jencarrington.

com/blog/2018/2/20/eight-mantras-reminders-for-when-youre-feeling-anxious-overwhelmed-in-your-business.

Gilbert, Elizabeth. Big magic. Bloomsbury Publishing, 2016.

Grabhorn, Lynn. Excuse me, your life is waiting: the astonishing power of feelings. Hampton Roads, 2000.

Hill, Napoleon. Think and grow rich: teaching, for the first time, the famous Andrew Carnegie formula for money-making, based upon the thirteen proven steps to riches. Organized through 25 years of research, in collaboration with more than 500 distinguished men of great wealth, who proved by their own achievements that this philosophy is practical. Sound Wisdom, 2017.

"Home." Jen Carrington, www.jencarrington. com/.

"Home | Anxiety and Depression Association of America, ADAA." Home | Anxiety and Depression Association of America, ADAA, www.adaa. org/.

DALE CARNEGIE. HOW TO STOP WORRYING AND START LIVING. AMARYLLIS, 2017.

Kondō, Marie. The life-Changing magic of tidying up: the Japanese art of decluttering and organizing. Leopard Books, 2016.

Losier, Michael J. Law of attraction: the science of attracting more of what you want and less of what you don't want. Wellness Central, 2007.

Luna, Elle. The crossroads of should and must: find and follow your passion. Workman Publishing, 2015.

"National Science Foundation-Where Discoveries Begin." Exploring the Brain's Relationship to Habits | NSF-National Science Foundation, www.nsf.gov/discoveries/disc_summ.jsp?cntn_id=126567&org=NSF.

Quisel, Heather. "Home." Heather Quisel, Feb. 2018, www.heatherquisel.com/.

Quisel, Heather. "Blog." Heather Quisel, Feb. 2018, www.heatherquisel.com/blog/.

Williams, Mark; Teasdale John; Segal, Zindel V. Mindful way through depression. The Guilford Press, 2007.

ACKNOWLEDGMENTS

Writing a book was so far out of my comfort zone and expertise. There are a few people I have to shout out for helping me make this book a reality!!

First, my husband who always supports my crazy ideas and adventures. Thank you for working double time with the boys while I worked on this. You are such an amazing husband and father. I love you! My boys who have taught me to relax, have fun, and enjoy life. You are my everything.

My parents, who have always been there for me. My Mom for being my rock during the hard times, for teaching me to never quit and live for adventure. My Dad, who gave me his creativity. Thank you for sharing your love of the outdoors. That is where I always feel best. Thank you to both of you for your love and support.

To my brothers who taught me to be my own person and not to take shit from anyone. My sisters-in-law, Heather and Kim, who are always there when I need someone to talk to. My friends, who always have my back especially Jenna, Leslie, and Lindsey.

My book mentor, Carolyn Colleen. I came to her with what I thought was a crazy idea. She provided me with the resources and guidance I needed every step of the way.

My editors Al Pahl and Lizette Balsdon. Debbie Lum for Formatting.

To Andy and Jenna at Jam Design who made sure my cover and website are perfect!

Thank you to everyone who has supported me on this journey!

A special thank you to everyone who helped me launch this book! I could not have done this without you!

ABOUT THE AUTHOR

Laura Mausolf and her husband live in Wisconsin with their two young boys. In her spare time she enjoys DIY projects around the house, reading, and anything outside! Laura currently works as an RN in the cardiac cath lab.

She has worked as a life coach for the YMCA and enjoys helping others. Her interest in self-help and personal development began after her own battle with anxiety and depression. After being unable to find a book to help mothers specifically during difficult times, she felt there was a need to share what she had learned with mothers everywhere.

If you would like to join the Battle Transformation Group or for more support go to www.lauramausolf.com.